Starting Your Business from Ground Zero

BY

NEWSAM T. MUTAMBA

First Edition, July, 2018

Printed in the United States of America

Petram Solutions LLC
Greensboro, NC
Phone: (336) 543 0187
Email: petramsolutions@outlook.com

NOTE TO THE READER

FOREWORD

Over the course of my 20 plus years of consulting with individuals, businesses, pastors and churches, I have found out that everyone regardless of their background has a dream. What differs from person to person is the condition of their dream or their plan to convert their dream into a reality. For the majority of people their dreams are nothing more than a wish.

As a retired CPA and business owner I am convinced that a business provides everyone the possibility or the potential to fulfill their financial dreams and goals. This book provides practical steps every individual can take to start a business and build the business the right way.

I highly recommend this book to everyone that desires to live their dream life by starting and building a business. I believe that "a perfected passion produces prosperity" and what better way to achieve this by turning your passion into a business. May God bless everyone that reads this book and inspire them to start their business!

William V. Thompson
Owner & CEO of The Church Coalition☐

1 WHY START A BUSINESS?

Are you living paycheck to paycheck? Do you hate your job? Do you see yourself retiring on your current job? Do you pay too much in taxes? Are you able to bless other people beyond your family? Are you wealthy (Robert Kiyosaki author of several books such as "Rich Dad, Poor Dad" states that wealth is measured by how long you can live an enjoyable and comfortable life without a job and without working)? If you answered yes to some of these questions, you definitely need a business!

Whatever your circumstances are, a business provides every person the opportunity to live an enjoyable and comfortable life. Secondly a business provides another source of income besides a job. Thirdly a business gives you the possibility to live your dream life! Someone once said we know people that don't know people," a business changes that. Proverbs 22:29 states that "Do you see a man who excels in his work? He will stand before kings; He will not stand before unknown men." What this verse is essentially saying is that a business can open doors for you & give you influence with important or influential people.

So what is a business? There are many definitions out there, from an Accountant's view point; a business is simply an entity with a profit motive, with owners/workers that work on the entity on a regular & consistent basis & keep good records of the activities of the entity. William V. Thompson author of the book "creating money without a Part-time job" defines a business as an activity you do for a profit, driven by systems and with the potential to fulfill your financial dreams and goals.

Now that we have established what a business is and why it is important to have one, we will take the next 13 chapters of this book to provide you with a blueprint on how to efficiently and effectively start a business. There are many ways to go about starting a business but this book will provide a simple step by step system on how to start your business!

Someone once said "the only thing that silences regret is pursuit". If you are ready to pursue your passion, dreams, goals etc... in the form of a business then adjust your mindset to an upright position, switch off all negative comments that told you starting a business was hard, because we are taking off on the journey to starting your business and when we arrive you will have a business that even the IRS and your State Government recognizes!!!

Michael Gerber in his book "The E-Myth: Why most businesses don't work and what to do about it" stated that when you build your business you should build it as if it is going to be used as an international Franchise. With that in mind:

Write Down your top 10 Reasons for Why you should start a Business, If your **WHY** is not Big enough you will fail...

1.
2.
3.
4.
5.
6.
7.
8.
9.
10.

2 OUTLINE WHAT YOU WANT TO DO (PASSION)

This chapter is designed to turn your passion into business form. As you address these 20 questions it will allow you to focus and direct your ideas into a business.

1. **What do you want to do? (30, 60 or 120 second summary)?**
   - You should be able to give a clear concise summary of your Business. For example: "Cash Flow U is an online resource dedicated to helping churches, businesses and individuals achieve financial increase through Bible-based strategies."

2. **Why do you want to do this business?**
   - Do you hate your job? Do you want to be financially free? It is important that your WHY is big enough, otherwise tough times and setbacks will cause you to give up and close your business.

3. **What goods/services do you want to offer? What Future services will you offer?**
   - It is not enough for people to need your goods and services but they must want them as well. For example: people need financial literacy but they are not always willing to pay for it, so it is important you research whether or not there is a market for your intended goods/services as well as consider what future goods/services you will need to offer to stay profitable.

4. **What are you passionate about?**
   - You need to be passionate about your business idea/concept or when things get hard you will quit. It is not enough to just be passionate about your business but you will need to work on it. **Perfected Passion produces prosperity.**

5. **What are the potential top problems you foresee for your business?**
   - You need to be able to identify the top problems you will face when you start your business. Remember "when you solve your problems you create money and when you solve the problems of others you create wealth."

6. **How & why are you qualified to succeed in this business?**
   - Luke 14:28 states "For which of you intending to build a tower does not sit down first and count the cost whether he has enough to finish it". In other words you need to do an honest self-evaluation of your personal characteristics and skills as well as your willingness to meet the demands of owning your own business.

7. **What's your story?**
   - Are living paycheck to paycheck? Do you desire to leave an inheritance to your children? Do you desire to fund the Kingdom of God? Whatever your story is, it is important you understand it and have the desire to change the ending of your story to your own desired end.

8. **What will your business look like when it is fully matured?**
   - You need to be able to see the end before you begin. You need to have the desired goal before you start, for example do you intend to sell your business, pass it down to your children, franchise it etc....

9. **Are you going to build your business as if it will be used for an international franchise?**
   - Being able to answer this question will affect how you build your business.

10. **How will you simplify your business for greater profits?**
    - For example a business might use a client managing software to track activities of its clients such as email responses, clicks on ads, web forms filled, purchases made etc... The automation of processes simplifies the business thus allowing greater efficiency.

11. **What is your business model i.e. your system for making**

money?

- For example an internet business might use landing pages to capture prospective clients which in turn are enrolled into a monthly subscription service.

12. **What are you an expert in that you must leverage?**

- Robert Kiyosaki defined leverage "as the second most important concept in the world of money". It is important that you identify your strengths and leverage them for your business.

13. **What are your weak areas?**

- Identifying your weaknesses is just as important as knowing your strengths. You don't want to waste time investing in areas you are weak in; instead you can leverage others in those weak areas. In other words you want to identify your weaknesses and then staff them or find qualified people to work in your weak areas.

14. **What strategic Partnerships will you need for your business?**

- For example, The Church Coalition has a partnership Agreement with a lending source that provides unsecured lines of credit to businesses, churches and individuals for any purpose!

15. **If money was no issue what would you do that you know would explode your business?**

- In order to harvest the best ideas it is important to initially discount money as a factor (solely for the purpose of brainstorming the best ideas).

16. **Are you going to automate your key systems? (Billing, marketing, sales, follow up, financial)?**

- The more you automate your business the more efficient your business will be.

17. **Which product or services will be the most in demand? Best positioned for growth? Best margins? Best future growth? Clients will buy out of excitement?**

- These are questions you need to be able to answer if you are going to be successful.

18. **What benefits should your client expect?**

   - If you don't know the benefits your clients will receive then don't expect others to see them.

19. **What is your unique selling Proposition (USP)?**

   - In other words, what makes you different from other businesses, or what makes you unique or better than other businesses doing what you want to do.

20. **How are you going to manage your life so that you stay focused on your business?**

   - There are many people that appear to be busy but accomplish nothing. If you are going to succeed in your new business you will need to maximize your life by practicing Life Management which simply means you optimize your daily schedule doing the most important tasks at your most optimum time and avoiding time leaks.

After answering these 20 questions you should be seeing your new business taking form.

3 DEFINE YOUR MARKET

Luke 19:10 states "For the Son of man is come to seek and to save that which was lost". In this verse Jesus clearly defines his market.

Defining your market allows you to properly target your efforts to the right audience. First you need to find successful businesses in the industry you want to enter (you will need to imitate before you can innovate) & then answer the following 11 questions:

1. **Who will be your market?**
   - You need to clearly identify your target clientele because different groups want different things for example millennials may opt to use Uber for a quick commute while baby boomers may call a cab.

2. **How will you best market to your prospective customers?**
   - Different customers shop differently for example baby boomers may use social media more on websites such as Facebook while millennials and generational Z may prefer instagram and snapchat. You have to market where your customers are!

3. **What do they want? Need? (It is critical that you know your market!!!!)**
   - Just because people need a certain product, it doesn't mean they want it so you must be able to distinguish between need vs. want.

4. **How do they want it?**
   - For example older people may prefer paperback books vs. electronic copies.

5. **What motivates them to take action?**
   - Is it value/cost, prestige/significance, group think (other people's opinion), peer pressure, quality, durability, aesthetics, etc... Whatever the reason, you need to know the main motivation behind your potential customers buying decisions.

6. **What keeps them from taking action?**
    - Just like the previous point you need to know what prevents your potential customers from making a decision to buy a product/service.

7. **What will you constantly do to keep your customers talking about you?**
    - For example an online business might create a community group on Facebook where customers share their experiences with the products.

8. **What are the unmet needs in your prospective industry? What are the over served areas in your prospective industry?**
    - It is a lot harder to break into an over saturated industry than one that is underserved.

9. **What will you offer your database to keep them engaged with you weekly?**
    - In this day and age of mobile devices, tablets, social media, the 24/7 News cycle, Streaming services such as Netflix, etc.... it is difficult to keep your database engaged on a weekly basis.
    - Weekly engagement can include using a texting system to send weekly text messages (92% of all texts are read within the 1st 2 minutes of being received).
    - Using an email service that allows you to send weekly mass emails to your database with feedback such as who opened their email, when they opened their email, who clicked on a link inside the email or what action was taken, etc....
    - Doing weekly newsletters.
    - Doing weekly Conference calls can be used for keeping your database engaged if it applies to your business.
    - Calling your prospects on a weekly basis.

10. **What will you offer prospects to obtain their contact information or to get them to call you?**
    - Offering something for free usually works for example free trials, free samples, free e-books, etc... The key is to offer your prospective clients something for free and in turn they will provide you with their contact information or even provide you with permission to call them back.
    - Sometimes just asking for what you want works, so don't hesitate to tell them that you want their contact information & why you

want it.

11. What key items must your website address to move people to action?

- Your website needs to be simple, concise and innovative, making it clear what you are offering, what the next step is, and asking them to buy your product, opt into a web form etc... (More information is under the Marketing and Technology Plan chapters).

Now that you have clearly defined your target market you can now build your business!

4 CONSIDER YOUR TEAM (STRATEGIC PARTNERSHIPS)

This is probably one of the most important chapters in this book. According to Les McKeown author of the book "Predictable Success". He defines predictable success as part of the growth business cycle where a business has consistently attainable and sustainable growth.

Mckeown states that size, age, money/resources, culture, industry etc do not predict whether or not a business will reach Predictable Success. According to McKeown the number one factor that determines whether a business enters predictable success is its **"PEOPLE".** So whether you are a one person operation or have several people working for you, it is important that you carefully consider your team.

As you begin to put your team together, you need to consider the following:

1. **Who will be your Board of Directors or Advisors that will provide insights for growth?**
   - If you are an S-Corporation or a C-Corporation you will need to assemble a board of directors that makes all the major decisions of your business such as approving the bylaws, hiring major employees etc.
   - If you are a smaller business such as a sole proprietorship or partnership, you still need a team of advisors that you can use to harvest ideas from.

2. **Who do you need on your team that can help you harvest ideas regularly?**
   - You need people with great life management who optimize their time, because busy people only appear busy but accomplish very little.
   - You need people who are more successful than you and have demonstrated success in their respective fields for example accounting, marketing, advertising, management, leadership, etc…. Even people in STEM fields may be beneficial advisors if they demonstrate great decision making skills.

3. **What does your business need to explode?**

- You need to know how to leverage other people in order for your business to explode for example a referral business model where people recruit new clients in exchange for a referral fee can be very lucrative when set up right.

4. **What will be your greatest obstacles? Greatest potentials?**
   - You need to be able to anticipate these.

5. **Will you be able to outsource services to companies who understand your market and can solicit business for you?**
   - There are times when you have to outsource services to other companies for example Cash Flow U outsources its marketing to a Marketing firm in Raleigh NC that is able to use its economies of scale and expertise. Another example, The Church Coalition is able to offer businesses unsecured lines of credit by outsourcing this service to a nationwide company.

6. **Do you have Profit- sharing programs?**
   - When you work with other people it is important to incentivize them, for example Cash Flow U members receive a referral bonus when they refer churches, businesses and individuals to Cash Flow U, and the bonuses are residual as long as the referral remains part of the business.

7. **How will you harvest your Staff's ideas?**
   - Daily or weekly brainstorming sessions are important for getting new ideas from your team.
   - It is important that when you initially start that you put very little restrictions so they can freely think of raw ideas.

8. **Will you Implement production or incentive programs?**
   - People are motivated by incentives and you need to find a way to encourage people to maximize their efforts. If people don't see how they personally benefit, they won't give it 100%.

9. **How will you help your team make money so that they can build for you assets you could never build alone?**
   - For example Cash Flow U has different people creating different courses which add to a powerful E-learning system that one person would have never been able to do on their own.

10. **How will you enhance you & your team's efficiency through**

life & personal financial management to stay energized, motivated and focused?

- You need to have daily "dates with your business future."
- Regular evaluation of your team to ensure they know what the benchmarks and expectations are.
- Match tasks to your team based on their passions and skills.

11. How will you keep the team in continual learning mode to stay abreast of industry & market trends?

- Major corporations have continuing education and training sessions, so should your business to ensure your team stays sharp.

12. When will you have regular brain-storming sessions with your team to harvest ideas?

- You need to create a culture where ideas are encouraged.

13. Are you & your team asking yourselves daily, "How can we improve?"

- You need a daily standard time that the team reflects on the Business.

14. How are you training & empowering your team?

- Pastor Otis Lockett Jr. stated "when people do not have the next step they stop." It is important that you establish training for your team such as continuing education training videos etc.
- It is also important that you give your team a certain amount of autonomy to ensure they are empowered to exercise their skills.

In Luke 5:2-7 we see Peter one of Jesus' disciples allowing Jesus to enter his boat and even though he had caught no fish all night, he listened to Jesus' instructions and launched his boat into the deep causing him to catch so much fish that he had an overflow and had to call his partners to assist him. The point of this passage is to reiterate that having the right people will explode your business like it did for Peter.

5 CREATE A SIMPLIFIED BUSINESS PLAN

Habakkuk 2:2 states "And the Lord answered me and said, Write the vision, and make it plain upon tablets, that he may run who reads it." In other words you need to have a written down simplified business plan.

The purpose of an effective business plan is to serve the following purposes:
- Focus your ideas.
- Provides a Blueprint for you to follow as you start your business.
- Creates benchmarks against which to measure your progress.
- Provides a document for attracting Financing.

Elements of a Business Plan

1. **Cover Page with Professional Appearance includes:**
- Demographic information such as the name, address and phone number of the business.
- Logo (if you have one) and the word "Confidential".
- Name, titles, and addresses of owners.
- Month and year the Business Plan was completed.

2. **Table of Contents:**
- Summary of the different sections within the Business Plan.

3. **Executive Summary:**
- One page summary of the different sections of the business plan (should be written last and is the most important part of the plan).

4. **Background Information includes:**
- Mission statement.
- Goals & Objectives of the business.
- Description of business etc.

5. Description of products or services:
- Describe type for example merchandising, manufacturing, wholesale, service.
- Describe features of products/services.
- Address property and proprietary rights issues.
- Describe Unique Selling Proposition.

6. The market plan
- A marketing plan is essential to your new business.
- You need to define your market (review chapter 3).
- You need to implement new marketing tools such as social media in your marketing plan (review chapter 8).
- You need to implement traditional marketing tools in your marketing plan (review chapter 9).

7. Management structure and organization:
- Describe legal form of ownership.
- Describe the chain of command (use flowchart where applicable) and the management team.
- Describe how the organization is structured (use flowchart where applicable) including a brief description of who does what.

8. Business operations:
- Describe Business location (address and why you chose location)
- Describe license & permits required etc... (Review chapter 7 for more information).

9. Financial Plan:
- Start-up costs.
- Funding sources (review chapter 11 for more information).
- Income & Expense Projections, Balance sheet Projections, Cash flow Projections.
- Describe Cash Flow plan (review chapter 10 for more information on how to do this).
- Tax Plan (review chapter 6).

10. Conclusion:

- Statement of feasibility. This is an assessment of the practicality of your proposed business idea with emphasis on such topics as cost and value to be attained.
- Action Plan. This is your to do list in order of priority.
- Supporting documents. This includes any other documents not mentioned that you consider to be important and pertinent to your business.

The Simplified Business Plan should be precise and concise so that you can easily study and analyze it on a regular basis. When getting started we advise you to keep it between 5 to 7 pages.

6 CHOOSING RIGHT TYPE OF BUSINESS STRUCTURE & HOW THEY ARE TAXED

Choosing the right type of business structure is probably one of the most important and consequential decisions a new business owner has to make. Why? Because the Business Structure you choose will determine how you are taxed.

Taxes represent one of the single largest bills most businesses have and so it is important that a new business chooses the right business structure. This will ensure that Cash Flow is not lost.

The first step needed in determining the right business structure is to do an Income/Expense projection & Tax Projection with certain assumptions. For Example:

Example 1: Income/Expense Projection of a Sole Proprietorship

Item (Projected)	Amount
Income	
Gross Business Income	$200,000
Expenses	
Salary	<50,000>
Business Office Rent	<18,000>
Electricity	<2,400>
Water	<1,800>
Part-Time Employees	<32,400>
Business Insurance	<1,400>
Trash	<600>
A/C Service & Repair	<500>
Office Supplies	<2000>
Supplies	<12,000>
Retirement paid by Business	<5,500>
529 College Savings Fund paid by business	<5,000>
Total Expenses	<131,600>
Income/Loss	**$68,400**

Example 2: Tax Projection- Comparing Sole Proprietorship to S-Corporation

Item	Sole Proprietorship	S-Corp
Wages	102029	102029
Current Net Profit	81600	0
S-Corp Income	0	81600
Employee Benefits	0	**(25000)**
Board Meeting Rental	0	**(9000)**
Other Fringe Benefits	0	**(16000)**
Adjusted Gross Income (AGI)	183629	133629
Itemized Deductions	(33600)	(33600)
Exemptions	(8000)	(8000)
Taxable Income	142029	92029
Tax (*20%)	28406	18406
Self-Employment Tax	12485	0
Withheld Taxes	(9500)	(9500)
Tax Liability	**31391**	**8906**

Explanation of the Tax Projection Example

1. In the example above you can see that any S-Corporation has deductible benefits such employee benefits, board meeting rental, and other fringe benefits that a sole proprietorship doesn't have, thereby increasing an S-Corporation's deductible expenses.
2. In the example above the S-Corp has a smaller tax liability ($8,906) compared to the Sole Proprietorship ($31,391). This is because of the many more deductible expenses available to the S-Corp.

Before we explore each type of business structure please review the table below on how each is taxed:

Taxation of Different Business Structures

Type of Entity	Type of Tax Return	Taxation
Sole Proprietorship	Schedule C on Form 1040	Entity not taxed, as the profits and losses are taxed through sole proprietor (owner).
Partnership	Form 1065	Entity not taxed as the profits and losses are passed through to the partners of the Business.
Limited Liability Company (LLC)	Not an entity in the eyes of the IRS	Use the other types of entities for Tax purposes. It is more of a legal entity for liability purposes.
S-Corp	Form 1120S	Entity generally not taxed as the profits and losses are passed through to the shareholders ("pass-through" taxation)
C-Corp	Form 1120	Corporation taxed on its earnings at the corporate level and the shareholders have a further tax on any dividends distributed ("double taxation")

A. Sole Proprietorship (Owner)

1. This is an unincorporated business independently owned and operated by one person. There is no separate legal entity.
2. Simplest form of business to establish and operate.
3. For tax purposes the profit & losses of the business are combined with the owner's other income sources (Schedule C on Form 1040).
4. Business seizes to exist when the owners dies or leaves the business.
5. Benefits include having one owner with complete control over management decisions and use of profits at their discretion.
6. This type of business structure may be best for people who have limited income from the business and mostly do all the activities themselves or just want a simple type of business.
7. Must file Schedule C with owner's 1040 Tax Return on an annual basis.

B. Partnership

1. A Partnership is an entity between 2 or more people who agree to

contribute resources towards the business and share the business profits and losses based on partnership contributions or Agreement.
2. In a General Partnership each Partner is liable for all debts, taxes and liabilities against the Partnership.
3. In a Limited Partnership there are both General and limited partners. Limited Partners have limited liability up to the amount of the investment made.
4. Minimal documentation is required such as Partnership Agreement.
5. Benefits also include the fact that resources and skills are available from all the partners.
6. Taxable income or losses are passed through to the Partners with Partnership paying no income taxes.
7. This type of business structure is great when you are in business with someone else, the income generated is limited and you want to keep things simple.
8. Must file 1065 Tax Return with the Taxable income or Loss flowing to a schedule K-1 that each partner files with their personal 1040 Tax return.

C. **Limited Liability Company (LLC)**
1. This is a separate legal entity for limited Partners.
2. Unlimited number of shareholders.
3. Benefits include lack of regulations imposed on S-Corporations.
4. For Tax purposes it is not recognized by the IRS so another business structure has to be chosen for tax purposes (or the proper term would be election for Tax purposes such as sole proprietorship, partnership, S-Corporation or C-Corporation).
5. Required to file Articles of organization with State. Yearly filing requirements (Varies with State).
6. This type of business structure is for someone that wants legal protection for their personal assets when their business faces legal issues & wants to keep things simple (This type of business structure is heavily marketed but my opinion is that an S-Corp is a better way of protecting your personal assets against litigation.

D. **S-Corporation**
1. Required to file Articles of Incorporation with state. Yearly filing requirements (Varies with State).
2. The entity must then elect to become an S-Corporation by filing Form 2553 with the IRS. An S-Corporation is a corporation that elects to pass corporate income, losses, deductions, and credits

through to their shareholders for Federal Tax purposes.
3. S-Corp needs to adopt bylaws.
4. It must be a domestic corporation.
5. Need to Issue stock to initial stockholders (Stock Basis determined by value of Assets Transferred).
6. It must not have more than 100 shareholders.
7. S-Corp can only have one class of stock but they can be both voting & nonvoting.
8. S-Corp needs to elect a Board of Directors and hold shareholder and director meetings.
9. Avoids double taxation unlike a C-Corporation.
10. Must file 1120S Tax Return on an annual basis with the income or loss distributed among shareholders (Schedule K-1) based on stock ownership.

Benefits of an S-Corporation
1. Liability Protection: Personal assets of its shareholders are protected from Business liabilities.
2. There is no Self Employment Taxes on Net Profit.
3. An S-Corp can raise large sums of money through the sale of stock.
4. Straightforward Transfer of Ownership: Interests in an S-Corp can be freely transferred without triggering adverse Tax consequences. The business continues to exist even if the owner leaves or dies.
5. S-Corp can rent owner's home for up to 14 days Tax free for meetings and deduct the expense (Rates must be based on fair market value).
6. S-Corp has a potentially lower Audit risk.
7. S-Corporation can have 501(c) 3 organizations as shareholders, thereby reducing the main shareholder's Taxable income on Schedule K-1.
8. S-Corporations can make charitable contributions to Non-profit organizations; however it is recommended that the amount not exceed 50% of Net Income.
9. Current Business assets can be leased back to the S-Corp while avoiding additional payroll taxes.
10. Current business owners can loan money to the S-Corp and receive interest payments on the loan while avoiding additional payroll taxes.

E. **C-Corporation**

1. Required to file Articles of Incorporation with state. Yearly filing requirements (Varies with State).
2. A corporation is a legal entity that exists under state law and separate from the owners and managers of the business.
3. Easy transferability of ownership.
4. Ability to raise large amounts of capital by issuing stock to investors.
5. C-Corporations are subject to double taxation (corporate taxes and shareholder earnings taxed).
6. There are more administrative requirements for a C-Corporation than those for an S-Corporation.
7. This type of business structure is beneficial for a business with heavy losses especially in the beginning stages because net operating losses can be carried forward indefinitely (previously 20 years).
8. Must file an 1120 Tax Return on an Annual basis.

After this chapter you should now be able to choose your business structure for legal and tax purposes.

7 LEGAL & REGULATORY REQUIREMENTS/CONSIDERATIONS

As a business owner it is your responsibility to ensure that your business is complying with Federal and state regulatory requirements. Failure to comply with governmental regulations may result in penalties being assessed against you and your business. It is also important that you carefully consider legal issues concerning your business in order to protect your personal assets as well as your business. The following things need to be carefully considered and implemented as you start your business:

A. Choosing and Registering Business Name:

1. You may name your business after your own name without having to consult anyone for example "William Smith Landscaping", however when using an assumed name such as "Smith Landscaping" you have to make sure it is distinguishable from other names by conducting a search with your county Register of Deeds as well as your Secretary of State to ensure someone else is not already doing business under the name you want.
2. It is also important to remember that there are restrictions with words such as bank, trust, mutual, co-op, insurance, engineering, architect etc (Check with your secretary of state guide).
3. In some cases you may need to conduct a search in the Trademarks registry to ensure the words which make up your proposed name have not been registered as a trademark or service.

B. Register your Business with Your Secretary of State:

1. Select the right business structure for your Business (Review Chapter 6).
2. Register your business with your State Secretary of State:
    a. Sole Proprietorship (owner) is exempt from this step.
    b. Limited Liability Company (LLC) files an Articles of Organization and once approved becomes an LLC for legal purposes...
    c. A Corporation (both C-Corp & S-Corp) incorporates by filing Articles of Incorporation. Once approved becomes a registered corporation in the state. An S-Corp has to take

the additional step of filing Form 2553 with the IRS and only once the election is approved does the corporation become an S-Corp.

C. Apply for Federal Employer Identification Number (EIN)

1. The EIN can be obtained from the IRS website. It only takes about 15 minutes to complete. The number will distinguish your business before the IRS (similar to social security number for individuals).

D. Apply for State Tax Identification Number:

1. The State Tax ID number can be obtained from your State Department of Revenue. It's used to distinguish your business for state tax purposes.

E. Apply for Any Governmental & Industry specific Licenses (if Required):

1. Special Licenses & Permits: Different industries have different requirements for example: a barber is required to have a Barber Examiners license, a building contractor is required to have a General Contractors license etc (may differ from state to state).
2. City or local licenses & Permits: Some cities and local towns require businesses to have local licenses and permits for example privilege license (right to operate in a city), zoning (some areas are not zoned for commercial businesses) etc.

F. Apply for a Business Bank Account or Separate Bank Account:

1. In order to apply for a business bank account you will need your EIN.
2. A business bank account or separate bank account allows you to efficiently keep track of business transactions.
3. A business bank account prevents you from comingling your business transactions with your personal transactions thereby giving you good documentation for your tax deductions.

G. Employee Requirements (If Applicable)

When people perform services for you they will either be independent contractors or employees. Generally speaking someone is an independent contractor when the business has the right to control or direct only the result of the work and not what will be done and how it will be done. On the other hand someone is generally an employee if the business can control what will be done and how it will be done (Go to the IRS website and review Form SS-8 "Determination of Worker status for Purposes of Federal Employment Taxes and Income Tax Withholding"). This form will help you in determining whether someone is an employee or independent contractor.

If your business has independent contractors there are things you will need to consider:

1. You will need to have all your independent contractors fill out Form W9 (exception if they are a Corporation). This form requests basic demographic information including their Tax ID number or Social security number.
2. At the end of the year, if the payment for services you made to any of your independent contractors is $600 or more, then you will need to send a 1099 Form to them and a copy to the IRS together with Form 1096.

If your business has employees there are things you will have to consider:

1. Employee Payroll taxes: such as Federal income tax, state income tax and Social security & Medicare taxes (FICA-employee portion) will have to be withheld on behalf of your employees. Employees must complete W-4 forms (Federal income taxes) & (state applicable forms for example NC5 in North Carolina) to determine amounts to withhold. FICA amount is determined by a legislative percentage.
2. Employer Payroll Taxes: Social security &Medicare taxes (FICA-employer portion) is also determined by legislative percentage (currently same as employee percentage).
3. Quarterly Tax Reports: 941 Forms have to be completed quarterly to report Taxes to the IRS as well as make tax payments, also applicable forms and payments are made to state tax agencies.

4. Federal Unemployment (FUTA) taxes: generally are paid by the business on the first $7,000 paid to each employee (see IRS website for more information on determination), same applies for state unemployment (SUTA) Taxes.
5. Sales and Use Tax: depending on your type of business (especially retail or wholesale), you may be required to collect sales tax. Sales Tax rates vary from county to county (Get more information from applicable state agency).
6. Workers Compensation: Workers' Comp is recommended for all businesses with employees to protect against the legal liability emanating from work-related accidents. However it is only required for Businesses with 3 or more employees.
7. I-9 Form: Every employee is required to fill out this form to verify their identity and employment authorization in the United States. This form is not filed to any government agency but must be stored by the business for 3 years after the date of hire or 1 year after the date of termination.
8. Send a W2 Form to every employee that worked for you at any time during the year.

8 MARKETING & TECHNOLOGY PLAN PART. 1 (ESTABLISH A SOCIAL MEDIA PRESENCE)

Social Media is one of the best ways to market your business while you are getting started since it is generally low cost and even sometimes free. In part one of creating your business Marketing and Technology Plan we will focus on the different types of Social Media.

A. FACEBOOK:

Facebook is one of the world's largest social media platforms with over 2 billion people logging in at least once a month. Facebook is the most important social media platform at the moment because of its ability to do all the things that other social media platforms do collectively.

1. Facebook Business Page:

A. A Facebook business page allows your Business to have a presence on facebook.

B. To create your Facebook business page >Click create a page and choose page category.

C. Provide Information about your business such as location, contact information, website etc under the About tab.

D. Add a Cover photo that appears on your business page. Make sure you choose one that exemplifies your business.

E. Add a featured video for your business. Makes sure it is short about 1- 2 minutes).

F. Review settings for your business page.

G. Set up events for your business using the event tab.

H. Begin posting to your business page on a regular basis. Post information about your business and show how knowledgeable you are pertaining to your products/services.

I. If you want to increase the reach of your posts you can boost your posts by creating facebook ads. This is essentially paying money to turn a post into an ad thereby increasing visibility by specific targeting of an audience.

2. Facebook Ads

• Create your Ad Campaign.

       a. Choose the objective for your campaign.

       b. Name your campaign.

- Create your Ad Sets.
  - a. Choose your audience.
    - i. Location.
    - ii. Age range
    - iii. Gender.
    - iv. Interests.
    - v. Other demographic information.
  - b. Set your budget.
    - i. Per day amount or Lifetime budget.
    - ii. Pricing-choose option that gets the most for your post at the best price- you are charged for each impression.
  - c. Ad scheduling (only works with lifetime budget)
    - i. Run ads on a schedule (Preferred).
    - ii. Run ads all the time.
  - d. Name your ad set.
- Create your Ads.
  - c. Choose your images/videos for the ad.
  - d. Choose text to go on top of the ad.
  - e. Choose Headline.
  - f. Review order.
  - g. Place order.
- Analyze the Results.
  - a. Review views of your ads.
  - b. Review the reach of your ads.
  - c. Review video average watch time.
  - d. Review button clicks (calls to action) etc…

3. Facebook Live:

- Allows you to broadcast information concerning your business live to the internet with your Android Smartphone, iphone, or applicable tablet or computer.
- To use Facebook live Log into Facebook with your username and password, tap "what's on your mind" at the top of your News Feed. Tap "Go Live".
- Write an optional description and tap the GO LIVE button. It will count you down 3-2-1 and then you will go live on Facebook. Tap "Finish" when ending broadcast.

- These instructions will vary depending on the type of device you are using or the page you are on. Preferably you will do it from your business page to promote your business.

4. Facebook Posts:

Making regular posts to your Facebook business page is very important and keeps the people that have liked your business page engaged. By regularly posting to your business page you will show how knowledgeable you are pertaining to your products/services. You can share your posts with others, For example, friends to tag people to the post (so it appears in their timelines).

When people like your posts, they have just become your prospective clients and you will need to follow up with these people. Facebook Messenger & Facebook Chat are quick ways to reach out to these people. You can also pose questions, take surveys or conduct a contest to keep these people engaged. Facebook posts are a good way to gauge how people are responding to your marketing efforts. Remember content is king, so make sure your posts are relevant to your business and products/services.

5. Facebook Groups:

You need to find 2 or 3 Facebook groups that have relevance to your business. You need to then share your hot products/services that people need within the group. For example, The Church Coalition would share its Unsecured Lines of Credit program. Also look for strategic partners within the group that you can do business with.

B. TWITTER:

Twitter is a social networking service where people interact with messages called "Tweets". Every tweet is restricted to 280 characters (formerly 140). Twitter is a great communication tool and there is no better example of this than that of US President Donald J. Trump's use of Twitter. Whether you agree or disagree with his use of Twitter, you cannot deny his effectiveness of getting his message across to his millions of followers through Twitter.

Setting up a Twitter account is simple; however, in order to maximize its effectiveness you must follow some basic rules. Twitter allows you to keep clients and prospective clients engaged, but in order to be effective you need to tweet on a daily or weekly basis. Tweet about current events, about your business, new products/services, industry changes, new laws affecting your industry, etc. (breaking news). Be original in your messages so as to attract new followers. Remember, Twitter is very interactive so you must be prepared to engage with people.

You can get people talking about your business and products/services by running Twitter Ads. The different ad campaigns you can run on Twitter are: Awareness (using location, demographics, interests, behaviors), Followers campaign (Increasing followers), Engagement campaigns, Website traffic (website card allows users to preview image, related context with call to action in their timeline, for example website link), and Quick Promote which allows you to promote a tweet by selecting target location, selecting your budget, and watching its metrics in real time. To summarize, Twitter:

- Allows you to keep clients and prospects engaged.
- You need to tweet on a daily or weekly basis to keep them engaged.
- Tweet about current events about your business, new products/services, industry changes, new laws affecting your industry etc (breaking news).
- Remember twitter is one of the main sources of information for young people.

C. Using Google for Your Business:

1. Google Business Page (Google My Business):
Google My Business gives your business a presence on the internet with a listing on Google. It doesn't replace your website but complements it. The information you provide will allow your business to appear on Google Search, Google Maps, and Google Plus. It allows people to find your business and products/services, as well as other businesses and products/services like yours.

2. Google Reviews:
An added benefit of getting Google My Business is that it comes with the ability to get Google reviews. Reviews on Google appear next to your listing in Google Maps and Google Search. Google reviews have several marketing benefits.

Firstly, they allow you to leverage other people in promoting your business. When people offer good Google reviews, they give your business credibility in the eyes of prospective clients. Secondly, Google reviews increase your visibility on the internet and may even enhance Search Engine Optimization.

3. Google Plus:

Google Plus is a social media platform created by Google. While it is not as big as Facebook, it still has marketing value due to the fact that there are over 100 million users. Google Plus works seamlessly with the other Google Applications. This is another way to market your business to prospective clients.

4. Google Hangouts:

Google Hangouts is yet another application created by Google that allows you to communicate with prospective clients through instant messaging, video chat, SMS, etc. This is a good, free way to communicate with contacts you have made within the Google environment.

5. Google Ads:

It's an online advertising service created by Google that allows you to be seen by customers at the very moment they are searching on Google for the products/services you offer. You can use Search Ads, Display Ads, Video Ads (YouTube), App Ads. The best part is you are not charged for displaying Ads but only when someone clicks your ad, views your video on YouTube, or calls your business. To summarize:

- In order to access Google apps you need to have a Gmail account for your business.
- Once you have a Gmail account you need to create a profile on Google Business. This allows you to have a business presence on Google.
- In order to increase your visibility on the internet you need to get Google reviews for your business.

D. OTHER REVIEW WEBSITES (Yelp, Yellow Pages etc):

- Creating an account and profile on local listings such as Yelp, Yellow pages, yahoo etc, will also increase your business visibility on the internet.
- Get Business reviews for these local listings as well.

E. YOUTUBE CHANNEL:

This is an extremely important marketing tool. YouTube is a Google Application and so when people conduct Google searches, YouTube results are included in the top results. When you have a YouTube Channel people are able to find your products/services **AND** hear your unique message.

A YouTube Channel gives your business a presence on YouTube. Your Gmail account comes with a free YouTube application. In order to increase your visibility on YouTube you need to get subscribers. One effective way to do this is to ask people to subscribe to your YouTube Channel at the end of every video. Having subscribers allows you to send them notifications every time you have new content, which keeps them engaged.

Depending on your type of business, you can get paid subscribers to your YouTube content by adding a link to a platform such as Patreon. This allows you to have exclusive content in addition to your free YouTube content. Tools such as Screencast O Matic &OBS Studio are a good way to enhance your YouTube content with different types of filters, widgets, etc. To summarize:

- Another great advantage of getting a Gmail account is that it comes with a free YouTube channel.
- Having a YouTube channel for your Business will give you increased visibility for your business because most people search Google or YouTube when looking for a product or service for example The Church Coalition receives a majority of church loan calls from people who viewed its church loan videos on YouTube.
- It is very easy to use and since it is free it is a good way to market a starting business.

F. PATREON
- This is an internet based membership platform that allows creators and businesses to run a subscription content service.
- For example if you have a YouTube channel or podcast, you can add a link to your Patreon page and offer exclusive content to subscribers or patrons of your content.
- Patreon allows you to have different tiers of membership for example $2, $5, $10, $50 etc… and they can pay monthly or based on new content released etc.

G. PERISCOPE:

- Periscope allows you to broadcast live videos.
- It is free and can be done using your Smartphone.
- It can be private (pay per view) and connects to Facebook/Twitter.
- It allows interaction between the host and viewers and is a good way of marketing your business to prospective clients.

H. INSTAGRAM BUSINESS PAGE:

Instagram is owned by Facebook and has over 1 Billion registered users. One of the benefits of Instagram is that it has easy integration with Facebook allowing you to post your Facebook posts and Facebook Ads on Instagram. You can upload your business photos and short videos to Instagram and use hashtags (keywords with #) to help people find them and find your business/products/services.

You can set up a business profile on Instagram with insights and analytics as well as the ability to turn posts into Ads. However, in order to take advantage of these business tools, you are required to have a Facebook page. Most users of Instagram are millennials and Generation Z.

It is important to remember that these other social media platforms are just as important as Facebook and Google in marketing your business and/or products/services. In marketing, you have to go where your prospective clients are, and increasingly these prospects can be found on Twitter, LinkedIn and Instagram. To summarize:

- Instagram is extremely popular with young people.
- It allows you to showcase your business and because it is linked to Facebook, you can post things from Facebook easily.
- Creating a Business page is extremely easy and free.

I. LinkedIn BUSINESS PAGE:

- The first step is to create a business page on LinkedIn (Marketing examples may change with time).

1. LinkedIn Sponsored Content
- Attract new followers to your Business or Showcase Page.

- Drives engagement with business-specific content.
- Appears on mobile devices, tablet and desktop.

2. LinkedIn Text Ads
- Great for generating prospect leads
- Add a compelling headline, description and even an image.
- Choose your target audience with precision B2B filters.
- Set your own budget and measure performance in the Campaign Manager.
- These ads are highly targeted and easy to create.
- There are great for budget-conscious campaigns.
- Ads appear on the top and in the right rail of many LinkedIn.com pages.

3. Sponsored Inmail
- Sponsored Inmail gets the right message to the right people by sending highly targeted messages – right to their LinkedIn inboxes.
- Use Sponsored InMail to drive conversions with more personalized messages.

Technology is constantly changing which means the way businesses market themselves has to adapt to this change. This Marketing and Technology Plan chapter provided you with low cost but effective ways of marketing your new business!

9 MARKETING & TECHNOLOGY PLAN PART. 2

In part two of creating your business Marketing and Technology Plan, we will focus on establishing the more traditional Marketing and technology tools.

A. **Create a Website**

It is a must for every business to have a website in this day and age. Your business website is the most visible display of your business on the internet. It all starts with a unique domain name that distinguishes it from other websites while still describing your business. For example, Cash Flow University has the following domain names: www.cashflowu.org, www.cashflowyou.org & www.cashflowuniversity.org .

Your website must tell the story of your business or organization. Most people will look up your website before they ever do any business with you. Your homepage should tell visitors what you do. It should be simple and concise. If people want more information they can click on links that take them to secondary pages. Your website needs tabs for different aspects of your business. For example, an **"About Us" tab, "Services/Products" tab, "Home" tab, "Contact Us" tab**, etc. See The Church Coalition website for an example of this (www.churchcoalition.org).

Your website should be bright with a colorful scheme, responsive design, and professional looking slides. There needs to be a **Search Bar** on your website, in case people need to quickly find something specific. Just like Google reviews, you need testimonials from credible people, preferably past clients on your website. It is also important not to forget to have a contact form that allows people to send messages to you about any questions they have. You can also have an email sign up link that opts people into your database of prospective clients (see example @ www.churchcoalition.org).

There should be direct links to all your business social media apps (Facebook, Twitter, YouTube, Instagram, etc). This allows you to link all your Social Media marketing with your website. This integration is important in maximizing your marketing efforts and converting your marketing into sales. It is also important that your website is mobile friendly because most people access the internet from their mobile devices.

Another key requirement for your website is Search Engine Optimization (SEO). It is important for you to maximize SEO techniques for your website so that your business and your products/services are visible in search engines such as Google, Yahoo, etc. Simple things such as having Google My Business & Google Reviews help in SEO. There are also partly free Plug-ins such as Yoast that will help optimize your web pages with SEO techniques.

There are many types of websites, from basic ones you can build on your own to more complex ones that require expertise.

If you are starting out and cannot afford to pay someone to build your website, you can do it yourself using a website builder that uses templates for example Go daddy's website builder product.

B. Email Marketing System

1. You need an email marketing system that allows you to email mass emails to your leads, prospects as well as current customers.
2. This will allow you to stay engaged on a weekly basis (You don't want to send too many emails).
3. An email marketing system shows you who is opening your emails, when they opened them, what links they clicked on etc.
4. An email marketing system also allows you to drip market your prospects by sending several emails in small sample sizes allowing you tell a story about your products/services.
5. An email marketing system allows you to embed videos, links, capture pages etc. This gives you a variety of ways to market to your prospective clients.

Content Marketing – sending out emails to your database with powerful information but not trying to sell them something. To your clients you are providing them great information so they stay connected and see value in what you do. To your prospects you are trying to impress them, to show them you are the expert and to build trust so that they trust you with reliable information.

Case Study Marketing – sending out emails to your database using a case study of an actual interaction with a client (true story without real name and with client's permission). The case study would show how someone used your products/services and how it helped them. The case study would educate them about your products/services and also show them the gap between where they are and where they could be if they used your products.

C. Texting System

1. Having a texting system is not for every business but if you are in a business that needs constant contact with your members for example a subscription service then a texting system is ideal for you.
2. Research shows about 97% of text messages are opened in 90 seconds or less, resulting in direct delivery of your message, unlike emails that have a lower open rate.
3. Segment people in your texting system into groups based on their wants and needs. **SPEAK TO THEIR PAIN.**

D. Conference Calls

1. Conference calls are another great tool to keep prospects and clients engaged with your business.
2. In addition there are several free conference call services out there such as totally free conference calls.
3. Conference calls allow you to have meetings over the phone instead of traveling to meet people.

E. Technology Analysis

1. Make sure you employ search engine optimization (SEO) techniques for your website such as a good website structure, internal and external links, a presence on Google, local listings, etc.
2. Make sure you analyze results from your websites, social media platforms, email marketing system, texting system with tools such as Google Analytics which allows you to track your prospects, members/customers across ads, videos, websites, social platforms etc.

F. Free Seminars

1. One way to market your new business is by conducting free seminars with a focus on key areas, products and or services.

2. Free seminars allow you to become an expert in your field or industry.
3. Free seminars also increase your name recognition and business visibility.
4. Doing a free seminar builds trust and respect with potential clientele.
5. You need to make sure you sell your products and services at your free seminars.

G. **Business cards**

Often overlooked, business cards are extremely powerful when implemented correctly. Providing your team with quality business cards and handing them out any chance you get will ensure that potential and returning customers have your information when they need it. The worst answer to "Do you have a card" is "I don't have one on me" or "We are all out right now" so make sure to print business cards regularly and be sure your team has some available at all times.

H. **Post cards**
Two-sided post cards with a simple powerful message distributed to a group of people who are identified as your target market. Make sure the card isn't too distracting & that they are able to carry it home with them since this is where they will most likely review it. Don't try to sell them on the spot unless you're at something like a conference with other vendors.

I. **Bandit signs**
When professionally done, with a simple but powerful message, these are awesome, particularly in a high traffic area. Be aware of local ordinances concerning these signs.

J. **Direct Mail Marketing**

Direct mail marketing is an old but still effective method of marketing when done right. Direct mail marketing is a tried and true way to acquire new customers. Services such as Every Door Direct Mail through Conquest Graphics can help you reach out to an area of your market that you may not have otherwise been able to saturate.

First, it is important to define your market and have a call to action in your marketing, as well as drive traffic online through web address, QR Codes, etc.

K. Apparel Marketing

T-shirts, hats & other fashionable wear are a great way to be seen & to start a conversation about your business. Satisfied clients can also wear the clothing.

This chapter contained the more traditional types of marketing and technology tools that are tried and tested and are guaranteed to market your new business successfully. While not every tool applies to your new business, you need to pick the ones that do if you are going to succeed.

10 CASH FLOW PLAN

Proverbs 27:23 states that "Be diligent to know the state of your flocks, and attend to your herds." This verse of scripture makes it clear it is important to keep a good accounting of your business if you are going to succeed.

Financial Statements are important because they provide stakeholders (owners, shareholders, creditors, investors, governmental agencies etc) with important information about a business. In this chapter we will look at a Spending/Cash Flow Plan, Profit and Loss statement as well as a balance sheet.

Cash Flow is the most powerful Financial Concept in the World at least according to Robert Kiyosaki. The success of your business will partly depend on how well you manage your cash flow.

A. CREATE A SPENDING/CASH FLOW PLAN (Budget)

The purpose of a Spending/Cash Flow Plan is to control spending and eliminate waste so you have more Cash Flow for your Business. More cash flow can be used to expand the business, hire employees or distribute more money to the owners of the business.

1. You will develop your cash flow plan by firstly determining what your business will need (expenses) on a weekly basis.
2. You will also need to project income by week.
3. Plan to conduct a weekly review of your Cash Flow once your business starts:
     a. Plan to Control spending by looking for waste on a weekly basis.
     b. Plan to Reduce or eliminate waste on a weekly basis.
     c. Consistently search for new sources of income or markets for your goods and services.
4. Plan to Conduct a Month-End Closing for your business where you will compare Actual Spending vs. Spending Plan.
5. The Cash Flow Plan example below has weekly budgeted Projections (Plan) & weekly actual numbers (Actual). This split allows you to compare your budgeted cash flow to your actual cash flow on a weekly basis (week 1, week 2, week 3 & week 4).

6. The Cash Flow plan example below has a column to your far right labeled Action Plan. This column is for notating your action plan based on the results of the comparison between budgeted and actual numbers. For example if your actual income is greater than your budgeted income, you need to know why and how to replicate the results. On the other hand if actual expenses are greater than budgeted expenses, you need to come up with an action plan to reduce or eliminate waste.

Review Cash Flow Plan Example in Table below:

Week	1 Plan	1 Actual	2 Plan	2 Actual	3 Plan	3 Actual	4 Plan	4 Actual	Action Plan
Income									
Expenses:									
Debts									
Operating Expenses									
Total Expenses									
Cash Flow:									

In addition to creating a Monthly Cash Flow Plan you will need to create other Financial Statements for your Business. There is several good software out there such as QuickBooks but if you are not comfortable doing it yourself you can always hire an Accountant to do it for you until you are able to do it for yourself. When initially getting started it is okay to use a simple excel spreadsheet as long you record your transactions properly.

B. Profit and Loss Statement

A Profit and Loss Statement is simply a Financial Statement that summarizes the revenues and expenses incurred by a business during a specified period of time for example a month, quarter or a year.

A Profit and Loss statement shows the overall health of a business by indicating whether or not it is profitable over a specific period of time. A Profit and Loss statement is a required document by lenders when obtaining financing.

Below is an example of an Income Statement:

Business Name
Profit and Loss Statement
For The Period Ended January 201X

Income	$11190.26
Total Income	11190.26
Expenses	
Computer and Internet Expenses	204.79
Gross Payroll	2883.24
Insurance Expense	200.00
Lease	636.00
Mortgage Interest	402.63
Office Supplies	501.51
Postage and Delivery	182.53
Professional Fees	130.00
Repairs and Maintenance	275.00
Taxes	916.04
Travel	236.00
Utilities	300.00
Total Expense	6867.74
Net Ordinary Income	$4322.52

Cash Flow Adjustments

Item	Amount
Beginning Cash	
Assets	
Debt Reduction	
Cash Changes	
Ending Cash	

Remember the Income statement looks at the revenues earned and expenses incurred during a specific period of time, while the Cash Flow Statement shows the actual change in cash during a specific period of time.

A. Balance Sheet

A Balance Sheet is simply a Financial Statement that summarizes the assets, liabilities and shareholders' (owners') equity of a business at a specific point in time. For example: the last day of the month, quarter or a year. **The Balance Sheet has to Balance (Assets = Liabilities + Owners' Equity).**

A Balance Sheet gives a snapshot of the whole business at a specific date in time. This can be useful in providing the owner with a big picture view of the business. A Balance Sheet is required by lenders when getting financing.

Below is an example of a Balance Sheet:

Business Name
Balance Sheet
As of January 31st 201X

ASSETS
Current Assets
Checking/Savings
Checking Account   25045.69

Savings Account	11772.32
Total Checking/Savings	36818.01
Total Current Assets	36818.01
Fixed Assets	
Building- Main	700000.00
Business Truck	5000.00
Computers	1000.00
Equipment	25000.00
Furniture	10000.00
Total Fixed Assets	741000.00
TOTAL ASSETS	**777818.01**
LIABILITIES & EQUITY	
Liabilities	
Current Liabilities	
Other Current Liabilities	
Federal Payroll Taxes	1414.81
State Payroll Taxes	354.83
Total Other Current Liabilities	1769.64
Total Current Liabilities	1769.64
Long Term Liabilities	
Mortgage	110901.66
Total Long Term Liabilities	110901.66
Total Liabilities	112671.30
Equity	
Retained Earnings	660824.19
Net Income	4322.52
Total Equity	665146.71
TOTAL LIABILITIES & EQUITY	**777818.01**

Note

It is important to make sure the Income statement ties to the Balance sheet. The Net income/loss from the Profit and Loss Statement flows to the Balance sheet and is added to Retained Earnings (review example above).

11 FUNDING SOURCES

The ability to get funding for your Startup business may determine whether or not your business will succeed. As a general rule you want to get 3 times of the funding you think you need. In this chapter we will go over several funding sources. While not every source applies to your particular business, find the ones that do.

2 Kings 4:1-7 tells the story of the widow woman who activated the law of recognition & the law of leverage by taking inventory of what she already had in her home (law of recognition) and then borrowing what she did not have but needed (law of leverage). The moral of the story is that you need to stop looking at what you don't have but look at what you do have, because it's what you do have that will create what you don't have but need. Secondly you need to look at your relationships and figure out who has what you need or has the ability to help you fulfill your potential.

The following funding sources will help you fund your new Business. Use the best ones for your business:

A. Owner's Savings
If you have enough money in your savings beyond your personal bill money, personal savings, personal debts, emergency fund etc then instead of borrowing money use your own money. Unfortunately very few people have the cash flow or savings for this option.

B. Informal Investors (Angel)
These types of investors are difficult to find but include family, friends, colleagues, private investors. You may find them by contacting your Accountant, Banker, Mentor etc...

C. Unsecured Business Lines of Credit
If you have a good credit profile (good payment history, good credit score, and low utilization of available credit) you may able to borrow funding for your business using an unsecured business line of credit. The Church Coalition offers unsecured Business Lines of credit between $25,000 and $150,000. The Unsecured Business Lines of Credit come in the name of your business and also give you the opportunity to build Business Credit with Dun & Bradstreet as an added benefit. You only pay interest on the money you actually use.

D. Credit Unions and Banks

If you already have a relationship with a Credit Union or bank, they may be willing to provide you with a small line of credit or Business loan. If you don't already have a relationship with Credit Unions or small banks then you should form one. Credit Unions or small banks are the most open to lending you money at lower interest rates.

E. 401K Loans

This is a fast and easy source of income on a tax free basis (provided you follow the limit rules as well as the repayment rules). Any interest charged on the outstanding loan balance is repaid into your 401K account.

F. Self-Directed IRA

You can borrow from your Self Directed IRA and legally pay no taxes however this is a complex and cumbersome strategy that requires expertise such as The Church Coalition Tax Strategists. For a simpler method, you can borrow from a traditional IRA interest free for 60 days.

G. Equity Loans/Lines of Credit

If you have enough equity in your home or investment properties, you may be able to get an equity loan or line of credit. However if you fail to repay the loan you may lose your home or investment property.

H. Loans from Life Insurance Plan

You may be able to borrow against the Cash Surrender value of your Whole life insurance policy. The Cash Surrender Value is the portion of the Cash that builds up in your insurance policy due to overpayment of insurance premiums.

I. Hard Money Lenders

There are lending sources out there such lending tree, Power 2 Fund that may be more willing to loan you the money you need but at higher interest rates than traditional lenders.

J. Shares of Stock

If you are a Corporation such as an S-Corp you may be able to conduct a private stock offering in order to raise capital fast, however you lose part ownership of your business when you do this.

K. Government Assisted Loans

There are several loan programs in which governmental agencies such as the Small Business Administration (SBA) will directly lend to small business owners or provide guarantee of repayment for other small business lenders. Research Federal, State, and local agencies for more information on these programs.

12 STRATEGIC PLANNING

Habakkuk 2:2 states "then the Lord answered me and said: Write the vision and make it plain on tablets, that he may run who reads it."

If your new business is going to succeed and flourish you will need to engage in daily, weekly, monthly, quarterly and yearly strategic Planning.

A. Date with Your Business Future

Your greatest asset as a Business owner is your time. It is important that you set aside a specific time period on a daily basis to work on your business. You should have a specific topic for every daily Date with your Business Future. Below is an example:

Day	Subject	Business 30 minutes per day	New possible areas to review
Monday	Marketing	Review your marketing options. Focus on the top 3 that are producing the best results. Even spend time learning about new options (Chapters 8 & 9).	
Tuesday	Cash Flow	Review your weekly cash plan & projections. Any deviations from projections? Any upcoming problems or opportunities	

		(Chapter 10)?	
Wednesday	Strategic Partnerships	Who do you need to connect with or partner with that will assist you both to grow (Chapter 4)?	
Thursday	Customer Care	How can you create great customer loyalty so that they feel a bond with you, buy more & refer more customers to you?	
Friday	Areas of growth	Based on industry trends what are the next 3 areas of greater growth?	.
Saturday	Study your industry	Imitate to innovate- What are successful companies doing in your industry to succeed (Chapter 3)?	
Sunday	REST!!!	Remember the Sabbath and keep it holy. Spend time with your family & friends so that you can recharge to advance.	

B. Simple Written Growth Plan

If your business is to growth you need a simple, concise Growth Plan that you have written down and that you can review on a weekly basis (It should be short preferably one page). If you fail to plan your business will eventually die. Below is an example of a Simple Growth Plan:

Areas of Growth	Example Business	Your Plan
New Sources of Income	Seminars, subscription membership website etc	
New Products/Services	E-books, CDs, new courses	
New Technology Tools	Texting System, mobile app, email marketing system etc	
New Customers	The increase in numbers of the same type of clients you already have.	
New Markets	These are different types of clients or demographic regions such as College students, single mothers, retirees etc	
New Marketing Tools	Textedly, Infusionsoft, Facebook Ads, Facebook Live etc	
New Team Members	These are people who work for you such as independent contractors or employees.	
Strategic Partnerships	Referral business partners, business strategic partnerships, marketing firm, accounting firm, lending source etc	

13 SUCCESSION PLAN

Isaiah 46:10 reads "Declaring the end from the beginning and from ancient times the things that are not yet done, saying my counsel shall stand, and I will do all my pleasure."

As you start your new business you need to have the end in sight. Do you want to pass on your business to your heirs? Do you want to eventually sell your business? Do you want to eventually turn your business into a Franchise? It is important that you think about these issues as you build your new business.

A. Passing Down your Business to heirs

If you plan to pass down your business to your heirs then estate planning will be very important to ensure they incur reduced estate taxes. The type of business structure will determine how you create your succession Plan.

A Sole Proprietorship automatically ceases to exist when the owner dies however with corporations such as an S-Corporation, ownership is based on Shareholders. It is important to speak to an estate planning expert to properly plan your business set up.

B. Selling Your Business

If you plan to sell your business at some point in the future, you need to consider the following:

1. Have 3 to 5 Years of Financial Statements (Profit and loss Statement, Balance Sheet at a minimum).
2. Have 3 to 5 years Tax Returns of the business.
3. Future business Projections.
4. Copies of all real estate deeds and/or leases.
5. Accounts receivable schedules if applicable.
6. Accounts payable schedules as well as other Debt obligations.
7. Inventory list if applicable.
8. Supplier lists including any contracts.
9. Customer/client lists including contracts.

10. Business organizational flow charts including decision making process.
11. Employee information and contracts.
12. Outline of business systems and processes.
13. Industry information available to the business.
14. A detailed Business Plan (see chapter 5).

C. Starting a Franchise

If you plan to turn your business into a franchise in the future then you should consider the following:

1. Your business should have standard systems and processes.
2. Incorporation will be necessary.
3. You need to raise capital for future franchise setup.
4. Standard Training procedures will be essential in your business.
5. Your business will need to have a proven business model.
6. Development of relationships with lawyers specializing in Franchises will be important in the research stage.

14 **CONCLUSION**

Starting a Business doesn't have to be difficult. In this book "Starting Your Business from Ground Zero" we have given you everything you need to start a business that the IRS and your state government recognize. This book was a simple step by step system on how to start your business.

You now have the roadmap for starting your Business. You have no more excuses for why you cannot start your business. Now all that is left to do is to.................. JUST DO IT!!!

JUST DO IT!!!

ABOUT THE AUTHOR

Newsam Mutamba graduated with a Bachelors of Science Degree in Accounting and a Minor in Finance from High Point University.

He received a Masters of Science Degree in Accounting from the University of North Carolina at Greensboro.

He currently works as a Staff Accountant assisting clients with Business startups, business registrations, Accounting, Tax Preparation, Tax Planning, Cash Flow strategies & other consulting work etc.

www.ingramcontent.com/pod-product-compliance
Lightning Source LLC
Chambersburg PA
CBHW071238220526
45468CB00002B/911